SHETLAND

Lerwick

ORKNEY

Kirkwall

H I G H L A N D

Stornoway

WESTERN

ISLES

Inverness

GRAMPIAN

Aberdeen

T A Y S I D E

Dundee

C E N T R A L

Cupar

F I F E

Stirling

Edinburgh

Glasgow

LOTHIAN

New town
St Boswells

C L Y D E

BORDERS

DUMFRIES &
GALLOWAY

Dumfries

SCOTL

9 Regions
3 Island Auth
53 Districts

SCOTTISH FARE

by

Norma and Gordon Latimer

Compiled and published by:
Norma and Gordon Latimer
2639 S. Van Buren Pl. Los Angeles, CA.90007
Drawings by Jan Dungan

ISBN 0-941869-02-4

TABLE OF CONTENTS

TABLE OF CONTENTS

TABLE OF CONTENTS

HERBS AND SPICES

Keep a good selection of spices and herbs in your store cupboard, for a well-flavoured dish is more interesting and it can tempt even a jaded palate, as it acts upon the taste buds and stimulates the gastric juices. Spices are obtainable in various forms, the most convenient being powdered--sold in drums--which keep almost indefinitely in a cool, dry place. Many herbs may be grown in a garden or window box. When fresh herbs are unobtainable, use dried herbs--either those you have prepared yourself or purchased in drums or packets.

TO DRY HERBS

Wash then after picking in hot weather, dry well in a cloth, then lay them on baking trays, padded with plenty of paper and a piece of muslin over the top. Dry very slowly in the airing cupboard or very low oven (with the door ajar) until brittle. Crumble then store in airtight tins or jars. In very hot weather they can be dried in the sun. Tie in bundles and protect from flies and dust by putting muslin over them. Parsley is a better colour if dried for a few minutes in a hot oven.

WEIGHTS AND MEASURES

Throughout this book, American weights and measures have been used.
For interest and for reference, differences between Scottish and American measures have been included.

SOLID MEASURES

SCOTTISH (AND USED IN CANADA)	AMERICAN (AND IN AUSTRALIA)
1 lb. butter or other fat............	2 cups
1 lb. flour.........................	4 cups**
1 lb. granulated or castor sugar.....	2 cups
1 lb. icing or confectioner's sugar..	3 cups
1 lb. brown sugar....................	2½ cups
1 lb. golden syrup or treacle........	1 cup
1 lb. rice..........................	2 cups
1 lb. dried fruit...................	2 cups
1 lb. chopped meat..................	2 cups
1 lb. lentils or split peas.........	2 cups
1 lb. coffee (unground).............	2½ cups
1 lb. soft breadcrumbs	4 cups
½ oz. flour....................	1 level tablsp.*
1 oz. flour....................	1 heaped tablsp.
1 oz. sugar....................	1 level tablsp.
½ oz. butter..................	1 level tablsp.
1 oz. golden syrup or treacle..	1 level tablsp.
1 oz. jam or jelly.............	1 level tablsp.

* must be standard measuring tablespoon
** ALL RECIPES USE SELF RAISING FLOUR UNLESS
   OTHERWISE INDICATED

LIQUID MEASURES

The most important difference to be noted is that the American pint is 16 fluid ounces as opposed to the British Imperial pint which is 20 fluid ounces. The American ½-pint measuring cup therefore, is actually equivalent to two-fifths of a British Imperial pint. While Canadian housewives use many American recipes and American measures, they are used to calculating in terms of the British 20 ounce Imperial pint. In Australia, 1 pint is 20 liquid ounces, but when measuring solid ingredients an 8 ounce cup measure is used.

SEE AT A GLANCE........

1½ pints.......3-3/4	American cups
1 pint........2½	American cups
½ pint........1¼	American cups
¼ pint........5/8	American cup

6

SCOT, SCOTTISH, SCOTCH?

As if they didn't have enough kings, lochs, bens and blens to confuse a visitor, they're rather insistent about what they call anything to do with themselves.

Harking back to that ancient Gaelic tribe (from Ireland), a 'Scot' is a native of Scotland. So is a 'Scotsman' or a 'Scotswoman.'

Almost anything which comes from or is typical of Scotland is 'Scottish,' as in Scottish hospitality, Scottish romanticism, Scottish thrift.

But when it comes to whisky, it's always 'Scotch' whisky (but a wee dram will get the message across in any Scottish pub). Also permissible: Scotch egg, Scotch terrier, Scotch broth, Scotch tape.

It all seems perfectly straightforward ˙ if you're a Scot with Scottish logic....

THE 'AULD ALLIANCE'

In 1295, King John Balliol (King of Scotland)
created an alliance with the King of France
to fight against Edward I of England to see if
they could beat him and weaken England.
However, the war between France and England
ended some years later and the 'alliance'
between Scotland and France was dissolved.

SCOTLAND
Cead Mile Failte

Scotland is a beautiful land filled with
romantic tradition and a tempestuous history,
where the clan tartans and bagpipes are all
very much entwined in their history and
tradition.

Scotland consists of approximately 30,000
square miles with a population of 5.2 million
Scots, covering the northern-most third of the
United Kingdom--SCOTLAND. It is a country
surrounded by the Atlantic on the west coast
and the North Sea on the east coast. Scotland
has some 300 lakes (the locals always refer to
them as 'lochs'). Included in Scotland are
some 790 islands, most of which are inhabited
by birds, but 130 are populated.

There are many fascinating stories about
Scotland but one we think is a touching story
is of GREYFRIARS BOBBY.

GREYFRIARS BOBBY is a true story about a Skye
Terrier's devotion to his master. After his
master died, BOBBY waited by his master's
grave in nearby Greyfriars Cemetery, Edinburgh,
for 14 years until dying of old age in 1872.
When his master died, BOBBY was in the eyes of
the law, a stray, and normally would have been
caught by the city dog-catcher and put to sleep.
He so touched the hearts of the people that knew
him they sent a petition to the City Council and
BOBBY was made a freeman of the City -- he
therefore had the vote long before women! After
his death the City erected a monument in his
memory.

THE SPIRIT OF SCOTLAND

No history of Scotland would be complete without mentioning whisky.

Whisky making has been in progress in Scotland for hundreds of years, or as some believe, at least since the Christian monks brought the skill of whisky making north to the heathens!

The word 'whisky' comes from the Gaelic 'Uisage Beatha' - water of life. There are two basic types: malt, distilled solely from malted barley, and grain whisky from malted barley and grain. Straight malt whisky is somewhat sturdier, primarily from the Highlands, which is the local favourite. There are more than 2,000 brands of authentic Scotch.

Although there are blends of whisky, the purist insists that single malt whisky is the true whisky and should be drunk only neat (no ice or other liquid) or with plain water -- never with soda, lemonade or ginger ale, and definitely not ice.

There is a complete ritual to Scotch Whisky involving pure mountain water, the aroma of peat and five centuries of expertise, all the way to the actual drinking.

An after dinner Irish coffee, using local whisky, may be called a "tartan" or a "Gaelic."

'Haste Ye Back'

A TYPICAL BURNS' NIGHT MENU

*Cock-A-Leekie Soup

*Chieftain o' the Puddin' Race
wi' a' the Honours
*an' wi' Chappit Tatties an' Neeps

*Bubbly-Jock an' Trimmin's
wi' Cranberry Sauce
*Stoved Tatties
Vegetables an' sic' like

*Tipsy Laird
or
Cheese an' Biscuits

Coffee

* recipes in this book

COCK-A-LEEKIE SOUP

Scotland has a great tradition of soup
making, or as more commonly known "Broth,"
of which Cock-A-Leekie must be considered
the national soup, although it is more like
a stew than a soup. Cock-A-Leekie is
believed to have originated in Edinburgh and
the Lothians. This traditional soup is served
on Burns' Night.

2-3 lb. boiling chicken
5 cups water
6 leeks, chopped
2 onions, chopped
2 oz. rice
Bay leaf, sprig of Thyme
1 tablsp. chopped Parsley
salt and pepper to taste
4-6 prunes, soaked overnight, halved and
    stoned

Place chicken, Bay leaf, Thyme, Parsley,
salt and pepper, in a large saucepan and
cover with water. Bring to the boil and
then lower the heat and simmer very gently
for 2 hours, skimming with a slotted spoon
from time to time when necessary.

Add leeks, onions and rice and more water if
necessary to cover the chicken and continue
to simmer, uncovered, for another 1 hour or
until the chicken and vegetables are tender.
The prunes should be added about 30 minutes
before the end of cooking time.

To serve, remove the chicken and discard the
giblets and Bay leaf. Skim the broth and
adjust seasoning if necessary. The chicken

13

can be carved and some of the meat returned to the soup and reheated before serving or eaten separately as a main course.

The prunes were originally added to 'sweeten' the broth if the leeks were old and bitter. Nowadays they are added by choice.

Serves 4 to 6

LORRAINE SOUP

The name of this soup is thought to have come from Mary of Lorraine, mother of Mary Queen of Scots

7½ cups chicken stock
2 cups chicken or veal, finely chopped
2 oz. almonds
1 tablsp. white breadcrumbs
2 hard-boiled egg yolks
lemon juice
½ cup cream
1 tablsp. chopped parsley
salt and pepper to taste

Mix the meat, almonds, breadcrumbs and egg, then add the stock. Add salt and pepper to taste and lemon juice. Bring to the boil then simmer for 10-15 minutes. Remove from heat and stir in cream, then reheat but do not boil. Serve garnished with chopped parsley.

SCOTS BROTH

1 lb. neck of mutton, lamb may be used
1 medium onion
2 leeks
½ cabbage
1 small turnip
2 carrots
3 oz. split peas
3 oz. pearl barley
10 cups water
salt and pepper to taste
2 tablsp. chopped parsley
1 teasp. salt

Place the meat, water, 1 teasp. salt and pearl
barley and peas in a large saucepan. Bring to
the boil and skim the top. Dice the vegetables
and shred the cabbage. Allow broth to simmer
for 1 hour then add vegetables. Bring back to
the boil and then simmer for a further 20
minutes or until vegetables are tender. Add
the parsley and salt and pepper to taste.
Other vegetables may be used depending on the
season .

Serves approx. 8

PARTAN BREE

Partan Bree is a crab soup and in Scotland
crabs are known by their Gaelic name 'partan.'
'Bree' means liquid. This soup is very
popular in the fishing regions of Scotland.

1 large cooked crab (2-3 lbs.)
2 oz. rice
2½ cups milk
2½ cups white stock or water
½ cup cream
Anchovy extract to taste
salt and white pepper to taste

Remove all the meat from the crab and keep the
claw meat separate. Put the rice in a saucepan
with the milk and a pinch of salt. Bring to a
boil and then cover and simmer until rice is
soft. Stir in the crab meat and the stock and
stir until liquid boils. Remove from heat and
put through liquidizer. Return to saucepan
and add anchovy extract and salt and pepper to
taste. Then add claw meat and heat gently.
Stir in cream and serve garnished with fresh
parsley.

FEATHER FOWLIE

The name of this soup was possibly derived
from a corruption of 'volaille' during
the Auld Alliance with France.

1 roasting chicken
1 diced celery stick
1 diced onion
2 carrots, diced
2 sprigs parsley
2 oz. ham
1 sprig thyme
¼ teasp. mace
3 egg yolks, slightly beaten
3 tablsp. cream
2 teasp. minced parsley

Clean and cut up chicken and place in
bowl and cover with salted water and
soak for 30 minutes. Remove chicken
from water and place in saucepan. Add
the ham, herbs, mace and vegetables.
Cover with 7½ cups cold water. Cover
and bring to the boil. Skim if
necessary. Simmer slowly for 1½ hours.
Strain the stock into a basin and allow
to cool. Remove any fat which may set
on top. Put stock back into a clean
saucepan and bring slowly to the boil.
Simmer gently for 30 minutes. Take
saucepan from heat and slowly add the
egg yolks and the hot cream to the
soup. Add the minced parsley. Remove
breast meat from the chicken and mince.
Add a little to the soup for garnish.

KALE SOUP

This is a soup common to the Outer Hebrides. The word 'kale' is used for not only the vegetable kale but also refers to any kind of greens.

2 lb. hough (shank of beef)
½ cup pearl barley
1 lb. kale or other greens
water
salt and pepper to taste

Cut the hough into small pieces and put into saucepan and cover with water. Bring to the boil. Skim off excess fat. Add pearl barley, salt and pepper and cover. Simmer for 2-3 hours. About 20 minutes before the end add the chopped kale.

TATTIE SOUP

With the abundance of potatoes and the excellent mutton produced in Scotland this is a very good country-style soup.

1 lb. neck of mutton (lamb may be used)
10 cups water
3 onions
1 carrot
1½ lbs. potatoes
salt and pepper to taste
chopped parsley for garnish

Put the meat into a saucepan with the water. Bring to the boil and skim off excess fat. Add carrot and onions, salt and pepper to taste and simmer for 2 hours. Add potatoes 30 minutes before the end. Remove meat from saucepan and remove meat from bone taking off excess fat. Return meat to saucepan. Check the seasoning. Serve garnished with parsley.

HOTCH-POTCH

This soup is also called 'Hairst Bree' - harvest broth.

1½ lbs. neck of mutton (lamb may be used)
2 onions, chopped
2 carrots, diced
1 medium cauliflower
1 yellow turnip, diced
½ lettuce
1 cup fresh peas
1 cup broad beans (fava beans)
1 tablsp. chopped parsley
1 teasp. sugar
1 teasp. salt
½ teasp. pepper
10 cups water

Place the meat in a saucepan with the water and salt and bring to the boil. Skim off excess fat. Cover and simmer for 1 hour. Add the onions, carrots, turnip, beans and half the peas. Cover and simmer for 1½ hours. Then add cauliflower cut in flowerlets, and shredded lettuce, the remaining peas, sugar and parsley and season to taste. Cover and simmer gently for another ½ hour or until vegetables are tender. The soup should be very thick.

Serves 4-6

Vegetables of your own choice may be substituted but they are best fresh.

HOUGH SOUP

This old Scots soup is very good on cold days.

1 lb. hough (shank of beef)
½ cup sliced carrots
½ cup sliced onions
1 small turnip, diced
1 oz. beef dripping
1 oz. sago
6 cups water

Cut the meat into small pieces. Melt fat in
saucepan and add the meat and vegetables.
Fry slowly until browned. Add the water.
Bring to the boil and skim off excess fat.
Cover and simmer gently for 3-4 hours. Skim
and then strain soup into a clean saucepan.
Add sago to soup. Quickly bring soup to the
boil. Cover and simmer gently until sago is
cooked. Season with salt and pepper to taste.

Serves approx. 4

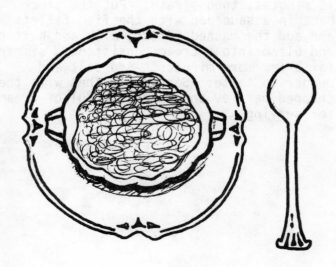

CULLEN SKINK

This is a very popular fish soup in
the fishing communities of Scotland. The
word 'skink' comes from the Gaelic and
referred to broth or extract, but is now
commonly used to mean stew-soup.

1 smoked haddock (2 lbs.)
2 tablsp. butter
1 cup cooked mashed potatoes
1 sliced onion
3½ cups milk
salt and pepper to taste
chopped parsley and cream to garnish

Place the fish in a frying pan and cover
with water, cover and bring to the boil,
then simmer for 5 minutes. Add the onion
and simmer for a further 10 minutes.
Take fish out and remove bones and then
put back in pan and simmer for further
15 minutes, then strain. Put the stock
back in a saucepan with the fish fillets
and add the mashed potato, milk and butter
and blend into a cream consistency, simmer
for a few more minutes. Add salt and
pepper to taste. Serve garnished with the
chopped parsley and a teaspoonful of cream
for serving.

Serves approx. 4

Scotland is a great soup making country with many soups to choose from, which vary from region to region. It was, therefore, very difficult to choose which ones to put in our cook book, but we have chosen what we think are the most popular and well-known.

The North East region of Scotland is the
centre of the fishing industry, with the
Herring being considered the national fish,
and Salmon being the gourmet fish. The
Salmon is among the best in the world. The
Shetlands also have a thriving fishing
industry with the fishing grounds of Iceland,
the Faroes and the North Sea within their
reach.

We have chosen a variety of recipes that
have the fish, or a close substitute,
available in America that may be used, and
recipes from various regions of Scotland.

TWEED KETTLE

This is an old traditional Scottish dish from
the Edinburgh area in the 19th Century. We
believe the dish got its name from the salmon
of the River Tweed.

3 lb. fresh salmon
2 green onions, chopped or
2 tablsp. chives, chopped
2 tablsp. parsley or dill, chopped
pinch ground mace
1¼ cups water from the fish
1¼ cups dry white wine
salt and black pepper to taste

Place the fish in a deep saucepan and cover with
water. Bring slowly to the boil and let simmer
for 5 minutes. Remove the salmon from the
saucepan and reserve the stock. Take the skin
and the bones from the fish and cut into 2 inch
cubes, season with salt, pepper and mace. Put
the salmon back into the saucepan and 1¼ cups
of fish stock and 1¼ cups of dry white wine
along with the onions or chives. Cover and
simmer for 25-30 minutes. Add the chopped
parsley or dill before serving. This can be
served either hot or cold with a cucumber sauce.

Serves 4-6

SALMON KEDGEREE

4 oz. rice
8-10 oz. cooked flaked salmon
2 oz. butter
2-3 tablsp. cream
chopped parsley
2 finely chopped hard-boiled eggs
salt, pepper and cayenne pepper

Cook the rice until tender and then drain
well. Melt the butter in a saucepan, add
the salmon, eggs, cream and seasoning and
stir gently until hot.   Serve very hot,
garnished with chopped parsley.

Serves 4-6

FISHERMAN'S STEW

This dish is a type of soup-stew served very hot and is the fisherman's version of Stovies.

1½ lbs. filleted white fish
2½ cups milk
6 slices bacon
1 oz. butter
2 lbs. potatoes
3 onions
salt and black pepper to taste

Chop the bacon and fry in pan with melted butter. Add chopped onions to bacon, mix well, cover and cook gently for 5 minutes. Slice the potatoes ¼" thick and add to pan. Cover and cook gently for 5 minutes. Season with salt and pepper. Add milk and bring to slow boil. Chop fish into 2" pieces and place in pan, cover and simmer gently until potatoes are cooked - about 20-30 minutes.

HAM AND HADDIE

2 fillets of smoked haddock
2 large slices of smoked ham
2 tablsp. butter
black pepper
water

Place haddock in pan with enough water to cover. Bring to the boil and then simmer for 2-3 minutes on each side. Remove from pan. Heat butter in frying pan and place the ham slices in it, then put the fish on top, and season with pepper. Cover and simmer gently for 3-4 minutes.

Serves 2

TROUT IN OATMEAL

Herrings may also be used in place of
trout. It is very traditional in
Scotland to serve trout in this way.

Allow one medium to large trout or herring
per person. Season oatmeal with salt and
pepper and then roll each fish on both
sides in the oatmeal. Heat 2 tablsp. of
butter, per fish, in frying pan and fry
fish on both sides until golden brown.
Serve garnished with parsley and wedges
of lemon. These can be served with oatcakes.

MUSTARD SAUCE

Mustard sauce is quite often served with
boiled or poached cod or other white fish
which probably has its origin in the Norse
influence. This is evident by many of the
Norse words still used in the Orkney dialect.

2 tablsp. butter
1 heaped teasp. hot mustard (English or
                according to taste)
1½ tablsp. flour

Melt butter in pan and stir in flour and
mustard adding a small amount of the fish
liquid used to poach the fish, stirring
all the time until it thickens and is
creamy. Add pepper to taste. Poached cod
with mustard sauce is often served with
Skirlie and Clapshot.

CABBIE CLAW

This is a Shetland Isles dish where the word
for cod is 'kabbilow' which probably has a
French influence from the Auld Alliance.
This dish can be served with an egg sauce or
a mustard sauce.

2½ lbs. cod
1 teasp. parsley
2 teasp. horseradish
2 tablsp. salt (sea salt if available)
1 lb. cooked, mashed potatoes
parsley and cayenne pepper to garnish.

Rub the fish with the salt. and leave overnight.
Next day place in saucepan, cover with water,
add parsley and horseradish and simmer very
gently until fish is cooked - about 20-25
minutes. Lift the fish out and break into
large pieces. Place on a hot dish and serve
with egg sauce or mustard sauce.

EGG SAUCE

1¼ cups milk
2 hard-boiled eggs
2 tablsp butter
2 tablsp. flour
1¼ cups fish water
pinch of salt, pepper and nutmeg

Melt butter in pan and stir in flour, then
gradually add hot stock from fish and milk.
Chop whites separately from yolks of eggs and
stir in whites and seasoning. Pour over fish
and garnish with chopped yolks of eggs and
arrange mashed potatoes around outside of fish
and garnish potatoes with parsley and cayenne
pepper.

HAIRY TATTIES

This dish is an example of yet another
useful way of using the abundance of fish
and is popular in the North East where
many of their dishes have a Scandinavian
influence.

1 lb. salted cod
1 lb. cooked and mashed potatoes
1 tablsp. chopped parsley
butter
½ teasp. hot mustard
black pepper to taste

Cut the fish in ½" slices. Soak over
night in water enough to cover. This will
remove some of the saltiness from the fish.
Drain. Simmer in fresh boiling water for
10 minutes then drain and flake, removing
any skin or bones. Boil and mash potatoes.
Add the flaked fish to the mashed potatoes
and season with black pepper, mustard, and
salt, if needed. Add the chopped parsley
and add knobs of butter. Place in a dish
and brown in the oven.   Serve very hot.

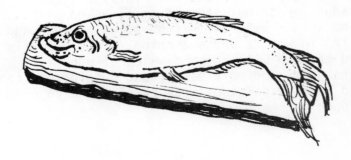

MUSSELBURGH PIE

Musselburgh has found yet another use for its plentiful mussels. If you wish to go to the expense, oysters may be used in place of mussels.

1½ lbs. rump steak
2 tablsp. oil
2 medium onions, chopped
1¼ cups water
1 tablsp. flour, seasoned
3 lbs. mussels
1½ oz. beef suet
rough-puff pastry to cover pie - about ½lb. or
                              5 cup pie dish

Cook mussels in boiling salted water for about 3 minutes. Remove from pan and take them out of their shells. Heat oil in a pan and cook onions until tender. Beat the steak until thin and cut into strips. Place a mussel and a piece of suet on each strip, season and roll up. Dip them in the seasoned flour and place them in 5 cup pie dish. Add onions and water, cover with foil and place in oven (350) and cook 1½-2 hours or until meat is tender. Remove from oven and allow to cool. Cover with pastry and cook the pie in a hot oven (425) for 30 minutes.

EYEMOUTH FISH PIE

Eyemouth is a pretty harbour on the East
Coast of the Border Counties. Here again
good use is made of all the fish that is
available.

12 oz. white fish (sole, cod, haddock)
1¼ cups milk
2 hard-boiled eggs
3 tomatoes, skinned
1 tablsp. chopped green onions

Sauce:
1 oz. flour
1 oz. butter
liquid from fish

Topping:
1½ lbs. mashed potatoes
1 oz. butter
2 tablsp. breadcrumbs
2 oz. grated cheese

Place the fish in a saucepan with the milk
and green onions and seasoning. Cover and
simmer gently for 5 minutes. Allow to cool.
Prepare the sauce by melting the butter in
a pan and slowly adding the flour. Stir
over gentle heat, then add the strained
liquid a little at a time. Check the
seasoning. In a 5 cup pie dish place a
layer of fish then a layer of sliced hard-
boiled eggs and sliced tomatoes, and continue
until dish is full. Beat the cheese and
butter into the potatoes, and spread on top
of the fish mixture. Sprinkle with
breadcrumbs and brown under the broiler.

SHRIMP PASTE

This paste can be served as an appetizer served on toast cut into bite size pieces.

1 lb. cooked shrimps or prawns
3/4 lb. butter
1 teasp. anchovy extract
pinch mace
pinch cayenne pepper
1 lb. filleted haddock or other white fish

Boil shrimp in enough water to cover them for 30 minutes. Strain the liquid, and then poach the haddock in the same liquid until cooked -- about 10 minutes. Drain the fish and leave a small amount of the liquid. Pound fish to a paste with the mace, anchovy and cayenne to taste. Let it cool. Then add 2 tablsp. butter and beat until smooth. Add chopped shrimps and heat together. Place in a dish and cool. When cool, melt the remaining butter and pour over the top then let it cool. To serve spread on toast.

Serves 6-8

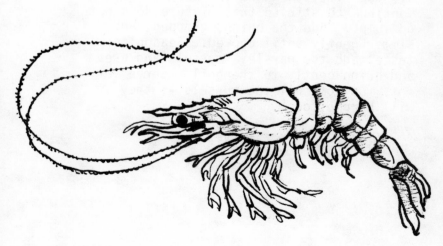

MUSSEL STEW

Mussel stew is very popular in and around Musselburgh which is famous for its mussel bed. Oysters, clams, or scallops may be used in place of mussels.

approx. 60 mussels
½ bottle white wine and 2½ cups warm milk
1¼ cups cream
2 large onions
2 tablsp. butter
2 tablsp. flour
2 tablsp. chopped parsley
salt and pepper to taste

Wash mussels well, and run through water to remove any sand and grit. Place them unopened in a large saucepan, add the wine and cover and bring to the boil. Let simmer gently for about 10 minutes until the mussels open. Strain off liquid and reserve it. Take mussels from the shells. Melt the butter in a saucepan, stir in the flour, then add the mussel liquid, stirring all the time, then add the warm milk. Continue to stir so that mixture does not go lumpy. Add the onion, chopped, and simmer gently until cooked. Season to taste, add the parsley, mussels and cream and bring gently to the boil. Serve very hot. Do not boil the mussels as they will become tough.

Serves 4-6

STOVED CHICKEN

This is a popular Highland dish which keeps all the flavour of the chicken. The Scots quite often stew their chicken in a closed pot rather than roast it.

3 lb. chicken, cut into serving pieces
2 oz. butter
2½ cups stock from giblets
3 tablsp. parsley, chopped
2 onions, sliced
2½ lb. potatoes, sliced into ¼ in. pieces
salt and pepper

Melt half the butter in a saucepan and brown the chicken pieces on both sides. Remove the pieces. In a saucepan place a layer of sliced potatoes then a layer of sliced onions and season, then a layer of chicken, dotting the chicken with small knobs of butter. Continue until all ingredients used, ending with a layer of potatoes. Pour over the stock and cover with a piece of greaseproof paper, and then the lid. Simmer for about 2½ hours, adding a little more stock or water if needed. Sprinkle with chopped parsley 5 minutes before serving.

STOVED HOWTOWDIE

This is an old Scottish dish using a pot rather than the oven for roasting and was probably influenced by the French during the Auld Alliance. The 19th century dish was served with poached eggs and was called "Howtowdie wi' Drappit Eggs.' The word Howtowdie comes from the French 'hutaudeau. Drappit Eggs means dropping them into water to cook.

3 lb. roasting chicken
½ cup butter
6 boiling onions
grated nutmeg
6 black peppercorns
2½ cups stock from giblets
2 lb. spinach
2 tablsp. heavy cream
salt and pepper

For Stuffing:
6 oz. oatmeal
1 medium onion, chopped
1 teasp. tarragon
1 teasp. parsley
2 oz. fat
salt and pepper

To make stuffing melt fat in pan and add onion. Cook until soft. Stir in oatmeal and season well. Cook for a few minutes, stirring occasionally. Add the remaining herbs. Add a little milk if mixture too dry. Stuff bird and fix with a skewer. Place 1 oz. butter in a casserole large enough to hold the chicken. Melt butter then brown chicken lightly. Add the onions, nutmeg and black peppercorns. Cover chicken with stock and put lid on casserole and cook slowly over a low heat for 1½-2 hours or until done. Meanwhile, cook the spinach in a separate pan, drain and keep hot. Remove the chicken from the pot and strain off stock into a saucepan. Add the cream to the stock and the remaining butter cut into small pieces, reheat, but do not boil. Place the chicken on a serving dish and put the spinach around the edge, and pour the sauce over the chicken, but not the spinach.

Serves 4

PAN WHITE PUDDING

This is a Hebrides version of Skirlie.

4 oz. dripping from roast
1 onion, thinly sliced
1 cup oatmeal
salt and pepper

Melt the dripping in a pan and then add the onion. Fry until onion is cooked but not brown. Add the oatmeal and seasonings, stir well. Cook for a few minutes, stirring occasionally. This may be served with stews, roast meats or game.

FORFAR BRIDIES

Forfar Bridies are a great speciality in
Angus, and on market day people come from
all over Angus to enjoy the Forfar Bridies.
They are the Scottish equivalent of
Cornish pasties.

1 lb. rump steak
2 onions, finely chopped
4 oz. suet
salt and pepper to taste
1 lb. short crust pastry

Prepare pastry and roll dough out on floured
board into four large ovals.

Cut the steak into ½in. squares. Chop suet
finely. Place the meat in a bowl with the
onions and suet, add seasonings and mix well.
Divide into four portions and place on each
oval. Wet the edge of the pastry and fold
each oval in half, crimping the edge with
your finger and thumb. Make a hole in the
top of each. Bake on a greased baking
sheet for 45 minutes. Oven 400F. Serve hot.

SCOTCH MUTTON PIES

These pies are popular all over Scotland.
In Glasgow they were called 'Tuppeny Struggles.'

1 lb. lean lamb, cut into small pieces
1 teasp. Worcestershire sauce
1 small onion, minced
½ teasp. mace
salt and pepper to taste
4 tablsp. stock
1 lb. hot-water pastry

Prepare pastry and roll out on floured board.
Divide pastry in half and keep one half warm.
Roll the other half out into a large oval, then
place a small jar in the middle. Mould the
pastry around the jar to about 3 in. in height.
Remove the jar and make another mould in the
same way. Roll out the lids, cutting them into
rounds to fit the top. Mix all the ingredients
together and fill the pastry moulds. Damp the
edges and place the top over the mixture and
then pinch the top on. Make a slit in the
centre to let the steam out. Brush the top
with milk and place in slow oven on a baking
sheet (250F). Cook for about 45 minutes.

Makes about 4 pies

HOT WATER PASTRY

4 cups plain flour
¼ lb. beef dripping or lard
1¼ cups water
½ teasp. salt

Place fat and water in a saucepan and bring to
the boil. Put the flour and salt in a basin
and make a hole in the middle, then pour the
boiling water and fat in and mix well until
cold enough to handle. Form into a ball.
Place on a floured board and knead well.
Divide pastry in half and keep one half warm.
Roll the other half out into a large oval,
then place a small jar in the middle. Mould
the pastry around the jar to about 3" in
height and about 3" across. Remove the jar
and make another mould in the same manner.
Roll out the lids, cutting them into rounds
to fit the top.

SHORTCRUST PASTRY

4 cups flour
8 oz. butter
¼ teasp. salt
cold water to mix

Sift flour and salt together. Add the butter
in small pieces and rub into the flour until
mixture is like fine breadcrumbs. Stir in
enough water to hold the mixture together.
Form into a ball, wrap in greaseproof paper
and chill in refrigerator for about 30
minutes before using. Roll out the dough
on a floured board. Proportions to make
one 9" pie crust.

NETTLE KAIL

This is a Highlands dish served on Shrove
Tuesday. Spinach can be used instead of
kail if you wish. When Scots refer to kail
they mean any type of greens and not always
the vegetable kail.

3 lb. boiling chicken
1 lb. nettles or spinach
10 cups water
salt and pepper to taste
1 oz. fine oatmeal

For Stuffing:
6 oz. medium oatmeal
2 oz. fat
1 medium onion, finely chopped
salt and pepper
1 tablsp. fresh mint, chopped

Make the stuffing first. Melt the fat in a pan
and fry the onions. Do not brown. Add the
oatmeal and cook for a few minutes. Season
with the mint. Stuff the bird and tie up the
opening. Place the chicken in a large pot and
cover with water, salt and pepper. Bring to
the boil and simmer for 1-1½ hours. Wash and
chop the nettles or spinach. About 10 minutes
before the chicken is cooked add the nettles or
spinach and oatmeal. Simmer for a further 10
minutes. Remove the chicken and place on a hot
plate and remove the nettles or spinach and
place in another dish.

COLCANNON
OR
KAILKENNY

In some parts of Scotland this dish is called
'colcannon' and other parts 'kailkenny.'

1 lb. boiled and mashed potatoes
1 lb. boiled cabbage
2 oz. butter (½ cup of cream may also be
             added if desired)
salt and pepper to taste

Mix the mashed potatoes and chopped cabbage
together. Put butter in a pan with the
potatoes and cabbage, and cream if used,
and season with salt and pepper. Stir over
a low heat until the butter melts and the
vegetables are thoroughly mixed. Serve very
hot with cold lamb.

RUMBLEDETHUMPS

This is a popular dish in the Borders and is
very similar to colcannon. Rumbled meant
'mixed' and thumped 'bashed together' - hence
the name.

Use the same ingredients as colcannon adding
1 finely chopped onion, chopped chives to taste
and 2 oz. grated cheese. Place the mixture
in a pie dish, covered with the grated cheese
and brown under the broiler or in the oven.
Serve very not.

CRANNACHAN

There are many varieties of this dessert and
it used to be served at Harvest-time or
Hallowe'en, with charms mixed through it.

2 oz. Crowdie cheese or cream cheese
2 tablsp. thick honey
2 oz. medium oatmeal
3 oz. malt whisky
½ cup heavy cream
4 teasp. clear honey
4 oz. of fresh raspberries, or any other fresh
           fruit in season

Place the oatmeal, whisky and thick honey in
bowl overnight. Mix the fruit with the cream
cheese. Beat the cream until stiff and put
a spoonful in the bottom of each dessert bowl.
Put the oatmeal and honey mixture on top and
then the fruit mixture. Make a well in the
centre and pour in the clear honey. Put the
remaining cream on top. Ice cream may be
substituted for cream.

Serves approx. 4

CAPER SAUCE

2 tablsp. butter
2 tablsp. flour
3 tablsp. capers with a little juice
3-3/4 cups lamb stock
salt and pepper to taste

Melt the butter and stir in the flour,
cook for 1 minute. Add the warm milk
lamb stock, stirring all the time to
avoid lumps. Add the capers and juice
and stir until creamy. Place the hot
mutton or lamb on a plate, cover with
the caper sauce and surround with
potatoes sprinkled with parsley,
carrots and turnips.

GIGOT OF MUTTON OR LAMB

The traditional Scots way to boil a leg of
mutton is with carrots and turnips and served
with caper sauce. 'Gigot' is the French word
for leg of mutton, and was probably introduced
into Scotland during the days of the 'Auld
Alliance.'

4-5 lb. leg of mutton or lamb
2 carrots
1 sprig rosemary
2 onions
5 black peppercorns and salt
1 bay leaf
sprig of thyme and parsley
milk to cover

Place the meat in a deep saucepan and pour
milk three-quarters of the way up the saucepan.
Add the onions, carrots, herbs and season to
taste. Cover and bring to the boil, then
simmer gently for 2-3 hours or until the meat
is tender. Remove the meat and keep hot.
Strain the milk and reserve 3-3/4 cups of
liquid for the caper sauce.

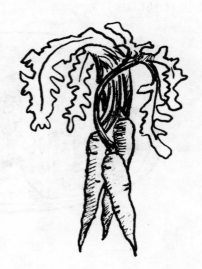

MINCED COLLOPS

This is an everyday Scottish dish and probably
regarded as being as much a national dish
as haggis. This dish is most often served with
mashed potatoes (chappit tatties) and turnips
(neeps) or cabbage. It can also be served with
skirlie (mealie pudding) which can be placed on
top of the mince and heated through.

1 lb. good quality ground beef
1 oz toasted oatmeal
2-3 finely chopped onions
1-2 oz beef dripping
1¼ cups stock or water
1 tablsp. mushroom relish or Worcestershire
          sauce

Heat the fat in a pan and then add onions
and fry until golden brown. Then add the
ground beef and fry until brown on all sides.
Season to taste and then stir in the oatmeal,
then add the stock. Cover and simmer gently
for ½ hour, then add mushroom relish or
Worcestershire sauce. Serve with sippets
(small pieces) of toast or mashed potatoes
(chappit tatties).

DUNDEE CAKE

Dundee cake is, of course, a speciality of Dundee, which is situated on the Firth of Tay. This cake is as well-known south of the Border as it is north of the Border. This is a rich fruit cake which keeps very well without losing its flavour. Dundee cake became very popular during the 19th century as a tea-time cake.

½ lb. flour
½ lb. butter
½ lb. sugar
pinch of salt
4 eggs
½ lb. raisins   ½ lb. sultanas
½ lb. currants
½ lb. mixed peel
¼ lb. glace cherries (candied cherries)
rind of ½ a lemon
2 oz. almonds, whole   ½ oz. almonds, chopped

Sieve together the flour and salt. Cream together the butter and sugar and beat in 3 eggs, one at a time. Fold in the flour, fruit, chopped peel, cherries, grated lemon rind and the remaining egg, together with ½ oz. of the nuts, finely chopped. Place the mixture in a well-greased 8" cake tin and put the rest of the whole almonds on top of the cake and bake in a slow oven (300F) for about 3½ hours until the cake is golden brown and firm to touch.

DUNDEE MARMALADE

The word marmalade comes from the Portuguese name for quinces - 'marmelo.' The preserve made from the quince was called 'marmelada.' Marmelada was first thought to be mentioned during the time of Henry VIII. The most well-known story for Dundee Marmalade occurred in the 18th century when James Keiller of Dundee bought some cheap Seville oranges and found they were too bitter to sell. His wife did not want to waste the fruit, so decided to substitute the Seville oranges for quinces in her preserves that they sold in their shop. The result was so popular that the Keillers continued making marmalade with Seville oranges. The Keillers have passed this recipe down from generation to generation.

Later on in 1857 in Paisley, Scotland, James and Marion Robertson devised a special orange recipe which they called 'Golden Shred.' Such was their success that they set up in business to produce the Golden Shred which has been passed on by generations of the Robertson family.

DUNDEE MARMALADE

2 lb. Seville oranges
2 lemons
10 cups water
4 lb. sugar

Place the oranges and lemons in a preserving
pan, add the water, cover and bring to the boil
and simmer for 1½ hours or until the fruit can
be easily pierced.   Remove the fruit and
allow to cool. When cool slice the fruit
coarsely, which gives the characteristic bitter
taste. Remove the pips and add to the juice.
Boil for 10 minutes then strain. Add the
coarsely sliced fruit to the juice and bring to
the boil. Add the sugar. Stir over a low heat
until the sugar has dissolved, then boil rapidly
without stirring, for about ½ hour. The
temperature should be 220F and the mixture
is at setting point. When the mixture is at
setting point remove from heat and pour into
warmed jars, and cover immediately.

Makes about 4 lb.

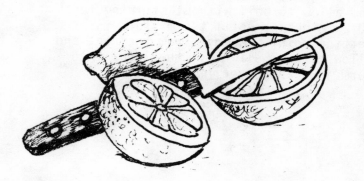

GOLDEN SHRED MARMALADE

3 lb. Seville oranges
2 lemons
1 sweet orange
15 cups water
sugar

Cut the fruit in half and squeeze out the
juice and strain, keeping back pulp and pips.
Scrape all the white pith from the skins,
using a spoon and put pips, pulp and white
pith into a bowl with 5 cups of water. Shred
the peel finely and put into another bowl with
10 cups of water and juice. Leave all to
stand 24 hours. Strain the pips, pulp and
white pith through a muslin bag and tie the
muslin bag loosely. Put the muslin bag and
strained liquid, the peel and juice into a
pan and bring to simmering point. Simmer
for 1½ hours until the peel is tender.
Remove from the heat and squeeze out the
muslin bag gently. Measure 2 cups of sugar
to each 2½ cups of juice and allow the sugar
to dissolve completely over a low heat,
stirring all the time. Bring to a rapid boil
and allow to boil without stirring for
20-25 minutes, until the mixture is at
setting point. Remove from the heat and
allow to cool slightly, then pour into
warm jars and cover immediately.

Makes about 8 lb.

GAME

Scotland is famous for its game, such as
venison, grouse and pheasant. The best known
venison is the Red Deer from the Highlands
which is at its best between October and
February. The Grouse is also very plentiful
in the Highlands. These birds are at their
best between August and December. They should
weigh about 1½ lb., which is usually one serving.
The pheasants come from the lower areas and are
at their best between October and February.
The cock bird should weigh about 3 lb. and
serves 3-4 people, and the hen bird should
weigh about 2-2½ lb. and should serve 2-3 people.
The hen bird is considered to have more flavour.
All this game is traditionally considered to
have a better flavour if 'hung' in a pantry.
The venison should hang between 2-3 weeks, the
grouse 2-4 days and the pheasant 10-14 days.

For those who wish to be adventurous we have
included a few game recipes. However, it is
not necessary to 'hang' the game as these are
available at better meat and poultry shops.

ROAST VENISON

Large roast of venison should always be
marinated before cooking.

1 haunch of venison (about 6 lb.)
2 tablsp. olive oil
2 tablsp. butter
½ lb. diced salt pork or bacon
salt and black pepper to taste

For the marinade:
2 cloves of garlic
1 bay leaf
1 large onion, chopped
2 carrots, sliced
1 bottle burgundy
1 sprig rosemary
2 crushed juniper berries (if available)
4 tablsp. olive oil
1 teasp. black peppercorns

For the sauce:
1 tablsp. redcurrant jelly
1 tablsp. flour
1 tablsp. butter
5 oz. port wine
gravy from the venison

To make the marinade, cook the onion and
carrots slowly in the olive oil until they
are tender, but do not brown. Place in a
large bowl and add the remaining ingredients.
Marinate the venison in this mixture for 2
days, turning several times a day, to allow the
venison to be evenly marinated.

To cook the venison, remove from the marinade
and dry. Combine the butter and oil in a pan

then add diced pork or bacon and fry until crisp.
Then add the venison and brown on all sides.
Remove the venison from the pan. Reduce the
marinade to half by boiling rapidly and then
strain it over the venison. Season to taste,
and cook in the oven at 325F for 30 minutes
to the pound.

To make the sauce, strain off the pan juices
from the venison and reduce them to half on top
of the stove. Rub the flour into the butter and
add this to thicken the juice. Stir well, then
add the port and redcurrant jelly. This sauce
can be served over the venison or served
separately. Serve with roast or boiled potatoes
and a green vegetable.

ROAST GROUSE

2 grouse (about 1½ lb. each)
4 oz. butter
6 oz. port
8 slices of bacon
juice of 1 lemon
salt and pepper
½ lb. raspberries or cranberries
sprigs of heather (if available)
          soaked in 2 tablsp. whisky

Place the birds on a baking tray and cover
with the bacon and heather soaked in whisky.
If the heather is not available you can still
use the whisky. Mix 1 oz butter, the lemon
and fruit together and then place in cavity
of the birds. Add the remaining butter to
the roasting pan. Cook birds in oven for
20 minutes at 400F. Then add the port to
the roasting pan, and baste the birds well.
Replace in oven for 5-10 minutes. Remove
the birds from the pan, take off the bacon
and keep warm. Reduce the gravy on the stove
and serve separately. Serve the grouse with
game chips, bread sauce and garnish with
watercress. Skirlie may also be served.

GAME PIE

1 lb. boneless stewing venison
    cut into cubes
½ teasp. ground cinnamon
salt and black pepper to taste
flour for coating
1 wineglass red wine or port
12 oz. pork sausagemeat
½ lb. cooked ham, cut into cubes
8 oz. puff pastry
1 egg, beaten, for glaze
½ cup jellied beef stock, warmed

Coat the venison cubes in flour seasoned with
cinnamon and salt and pepper and then put in
a casserole, with a funnel in the middle. Stir
in the red wine or port, cover and cook in a
moderate oven (350F) for 1½-2 hours or until
the venison is tender. Put ½ the sausagemeat
in a 3-4 pint pie dish. Mix the ham into the
venison mixture and put this on top of the
sausagemeat, then finish with a layer of
sausagemeat. Prepare the pastry and cover the
pie, and making a hole in the middle of the
pastry for the funnel. Brush with the beaten
egg. Bake in a fairly hot oven (400F) for
30 minutes or until the pastry is golden-brown.
Remove pie from oven and gradually pour the
beef stock into the pie through the funnel,
being careful that it does not overflow.

ROAST PHEASANT

Pheasant is a very flavourful dish and the
pheasant season is from October to February.
Pheasant should be served with bread sauce
and game chips and garnished with watercress.
The hen bird is considered better flavoured
and usually weighs 2-2½ lb.

To cook, first wash the pheasant, then melt
the butter and rub both inside and outside of
the bird with the melted butter. Squeeze a
little lemon juice both inside and outside of
the bird. Then salt and pepper both inside
and outside. Place leg side down in a roasting
pan and put in the oven at 375F for 15-20
minutes. Turn over on the other leg and cook
for another 15-20 minutes, basting frequently.
Turn the bird on its back, cover the breast
with strips of bacon and roast for a final
15-20 minutes. Remove the bacon for a few
minutes at the end to brown the breast. Place
the bird on a heated serving dish and leave for
10 minutes in a warm place before carving.

To make a gravy, use 1½ cups of water or game
stock and 3 tablsp. port or red wine, salt and
pepper to taste. Use some of the scrapings
from the roasting pan for added flavour.

CUSTARD

2 egg yolks
¼ cup sugar
1¼ cups milk
1½ tablsp. cornstarch
¼ cup milk
1 teasp. vanilla

Beat until creamy the egg yolks and sugar.
Scald the 1¼ cups milk and then pour over
the yolk mixture. Dissolve the cornstarch
in the ¼ cup milk and then stir this into
the yolk mixture. Stir and cook these
ingredients over a very low heat until
they are thick. Cool them slightly then
add the vanilla.

BRIDE'S BONN

This is a traditional bridal cake from the Orkney and Shetland region. It should be made and eaten the same day.

1 cup self-raising flour
3 oz. butter
1 oz. caster sugar
½ teasp. caraway seeds
milk to mix

Sift flour in a bowl and then rub in the butter. Add the caraway and sugar. Mix in the milk to make a soft dough. Place on a floured board and press out lightly into a round about 3/4" thick. Divide into four quarters and put on a hot girdle. Bake for 5 minutes on both sides.

ROASTIT BUBBLY-JOCK

1 turkey, about 12 lb.
5 tablsp. poultry dripping
2 oz. melted butter
1 lb. sausage meat
1 tablsp. redcurrant or cranberry jelly
2½ cups giblet stock
salt and pepper

For Stuffing:
1 cup breadcrumbs
6 oysters
8 chestnuts
1 celery heart, chopped
½ cup milk
chopped turkey liver
1 teasp. chopped parsley

To make the stuffing soak the breadcrumbs in
the milk and then combine all of the other
ingredients. Stuff the body of the turkey
with this mixture. Place the sausage meat
in the neck opening of the turkey and tie.
Place the turkey in a roasting tin and brush
with the melted butter. Place the dripping
around the turkey, cover with foil and roast
in a moderate oven (300F) 20-25 minutes to the
pound. Baste during cooking and season with
salt and pepper. When cooked remove turkey
to warm dish. Pour off excess fat from pan
and add the giblet stock and redcurrant jelly.
Season to taste, bring to a rapid boil to
reduce sauce. Serve sauce separately.
Serve with Stoved Tatties and vegetables of
your choice.

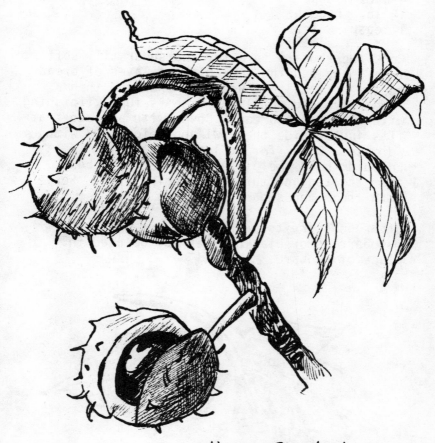

Horse Chestnut.

DRUMLANRIG PUDDING

This pudding is very similar to the English summer pudding, and it got its name from Drumlanrig Castle in Dumfriesshire.

8 oz. sliced, crustless stale white bread, cut
           into ½" thick slices
4-6 oz. sugar
1½ lb. rhubarb
1 teasp. water

Cook the rhubarb in water and sugar till soft. In a 5 cup pudding bowl place a layer of bread on the bottom, then add some rhubarb, then a layer of bread until the dish is full, finishing with a layer of bread. Cover with a plate that fits just inside the bowl and weigh down with weights. Chill for at least 24 hours. To unmould, hold the plate and invert the bowl over the top and turn the pudding over. Serve with cream and sugar.

Other soft fruits such as redcurrants, raspberries or blackberries may be used in place of rhubarb.

BORDER TART

For the pastry:
1 cup plain flour
2½ oz. butter
1 oz. sugar
1 egg yolk

For the filling:
2 oz. butter
2 oz. sugar
2 oz. self-raising flour
2 eggs
2 tablsp. raspberry jam
½ oz. flaked almonds
1 oz. ground almonds

Make up the pastry and roll out on floured board to line an 8" flan ring. Keep the scraps and roll out to make strips for the lattice design on top of the tart.

To make the filling beat the sugar and butter together until the mixture becomes creamy. Add the sifted flour and ground almonds. Spread a layer of jam over the bottom of the pastry and then add the filling. Arrange a lattice design of pastry strips on top. Cover with the flaked almonds. Bake in moderate oven (350F) for 30 minutes. 15 minutes before the tart is cooked remove from oven and sprinkle over a layer of confectioner's sugar. Return to oven. Serve with fresh cream.

ECCLEFECHAN BUTTER TART

This is another version of the Border Tart. Use the same ingredients for the pastry and make up in the same manner.

For the Filling:
3 oz. brown sugar
2 oz. melted butter
1 egg
½ cup mixed dried fruit
1 oz. chopped walnuts
2 teasp. wine vinegar

Having prepared the pastry in the same manner
as the Border Tart, now mix the butter, eggs
and sugar together then stir in the vinegar,
nuts and mixed dried fruit. Pour this
mixture into the pastry case and bake for
30 minutes in an oven (375F). This can be
served hot or cold, with cream.

FOCHABERS GINGERBREAD

This is a lovely rich gingerbread mixed with beer.

½ cup treacle (molasses)
1 egg
½ cup currants and sultanas, mixed
2 oz. candied peel
½ cup butter and 2 oz. sugar
2 cups flour
1 teasp. ground cloves
1 teasp. baking soda
1 teasp. each of cinnamon, mixed spice and
        ginger
5 oz. dark beer

Blend the butter and sugar to a cream. Warm the treacle and then add to the butter and sugar. Then beat the eggs and add them one at a time to the mixture. Mix together in a separate bowl the flour, fruit and all the spices. Then add to the butter mixture. Dissolve the baking soda in the beer and add to the mixture. Mix all ingredients thoroughly. Place mixture in a greased 1 lb. size loaf tin and bake in moderate oven (300F) for 1 hour. Remove from the loaf tin and leave to cool on wire rack. Slice and serve.

STRATHBOGIE MIST

½ cup sugar
juice of 1 lemon
8 pear halves (tinned)
grated rind of 1 lemon
2½ cups heavy cream
5 oz. ginger wine

Break pears into small pieces and place in bottom of dessert bowl. Stir together the sugar, lemon juice, rind and ginger wine until the sugar has dissolved. Add the cream and whip slightly. Pile on top of the pears and serve chilled. Other fruit of your choice may be substituted for the pears.

Serves 4

DRAMBUIE FLUMMERY

2 egg yolks
4 teasp. sugar
½ cup Drambuie
½ cup lightly whipped cream
4 teasp. water

Put the water, sugar and eggs in a double boiler, and beat the eggs over a low heat until a 'ribbon' stage is reached. Allow the eggs to cool slightly, then add the Drambuie, return to heat and bring back to 'ribbon' stage. Allow to cool, then slowly add the cream, folding gently. Serve with shortbread.

Serves 3-4

MIDLOTHIAN OATCAKES

Oatcakes like shortbread are made in many different varieties but this recipe is a favourite around Edinburgh and the Lothians.

½ cup plain flour
1 cup medium oatmeal
3 oz. butter
1 teasp. baking powder
½ teasp. salt
water to mix

Place flour, oatmeal, baking powder and salt in a bowl. Melt the butter. Make a well in the centre of the flour mixture and add the melted butter and enough water to make a stiff dough. Roll out the dough on a floured board and cut into rounds about 2½ ins. in diameter. Bake in a warm oven (300F) for 30 minutes.

HIGHLAND OATCAKES

Unlike the Lowlanders, the Highlanders would never use two kinds of grain. Their oatcakes are always made with oatmeal only, with a little less fat and water, making them brittle.

½ cup oatmeal
¼ oz. butter
pinch of baking soda
pinch of salt
water to mix

Place oatmeal in a bowl and make a well in the centre. Melt the fat in boiling water (3 tablsp.) and then pour into oatmeal and mix to a stiff dough. Roll dough out on floured board. Roll into a round about 1/8 in. thick. Cut into farls (quarters) and bake slowly on a girdle

until they harden and the corners turn up
at the edges. To serve place in a cool
oven for about 30 minutes until warm.

BONNACH IMEACH

This is an oatcake from the Hebrides which
is much thicker and heavier than oatcakes
from other regions. The Gaelic name means
cake with butter.

1½ cups medium oatmeal
1 egg
½ cup hot milk
½ oz. butter

Place the oatmeal in a bowl and add the
salt and butter. Make a well in the centre
and add the egg and milk. Mix to a fairly
stiff dough. Roll out on floured board
about ¼ in. thick into a large round and cut
into triangles and bake about 5 minutes on
both sides on a hot girdle. Cool and serve
with butter and honey.

SELKIRK BANNOCK

The Selkirk Bannock is the most famous of the various types of bannocks. It is a yeast bun, shaped like a round loaf, which is filled with sultanas. Bannocks are thicker than oatcakes and are usually cut into quarters.

2 lb. plain flour
½ cup lard
½ cup butter
1 cup sugar
1 lb. sultanas or raisins
1 oz. yeast
15 oz. milk
milk and sugar for glazing
pinch of salt

Sift flour into a bowl, add a pinch of salt and leave in a warm place. Cream the yeast with 1 teasp. sugar. Melt butter and lard in a pan then add milk and allow to cool until it is just warm. Make a well in the centre of the flour and add the milk mixture and yeast. Mix to a soft dough then knead on a floured board for 5 minutes. Leave in a bowl covered with a damp cloth in a warm place until it has doubled in size. Turn the dough onto a floured board and mix in the sugar and dried fruit. Shape into four rounds and place on greased baking sheet and leave in a warm place until they have risen, about 20-30 minutes. Put in hot oven (425F) for 15 minutes, then reduce heat to 375F and bake until golden brown, about 25-30 minutes. Warm a little milk with 1 tablsp. sugar and glaze the top of the bannocks about 15 minutes before they are ready.

PETTICOAT TAILS

Although there are many different shortbreads
this particular one is from the Edinburgh
region where it got its name from the
petticoat hoops worn by the 19th century
ladies. Yet another story is that Mary Queen
of Scots was very fond of this shortbread and
Petticoat Tails is a corruption of the French
word 'petites gatelles,' - little cakes.

1½ cups flour
3 tablsp. sugar
3/4 cup butter
4 tablsp. milk
2 teasp. caraway (optional)

Mix the caraway seeds, if used, with the flour.
Melt the butter in the milk, then make a well
in the centre of the flour and pour in the
milk mixture and then the sugar. Mix well, and
knead lightly. Place on a floured board and
roll out to ¼ in. thickness, into a circle.
Place on a greased baking sheet and then crimp
the edges with your finger and thumb. Then
prick all over with a fork. Cut across the
circle diagonally into 8 pieces. Do not cut
through the paste, but make a deep incision.
Place in a moderate oven (350F) for 20 minutes,
or until crisp and golden. Cool on a wire
rack, and dust with sugar. Break the circle
in the 8 pieces as marked, and serve.

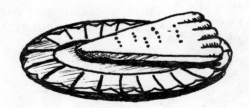

ORKNEY BROONIES

This Orkney Broonie is a traditional oatmeal gingerbread. The word 'broonie' means a thick bannock and comes from the Norse 'bruni.' This broonie is rather like the English Parkin.

1 cup fine oatmeal
½ cup self-raising flour
2 teasp. ground ginger
½ cup butter
5 oz. golden syrup (corn syrup)
2 oz. black treacle (molasses)
½ cup light brown sugar
½ teasp. baking soda
5 oz. buttermilk
1 egg
pinch of salt

Mix the oatmeal and flour together and rub in the butter, then add the salt, sugar, soda and ginger. Mix the treacle, golden syrup, buttermilk and egg together and then add to the dry ingredients to make a soft consistency. Pour into a greased 8" square tin and bake for 35 minutes at 350F. These should be kept in an airtight tin for about a week for a better flavour.

BLACK BUN

Black Bun is a rich fruit cake which was
eaten on Twelfth Night, but is now served
at Hogmanay. Like a Christmas cake, this
should be made several weeks before it is
required, so that it can mature.

8 oz. shortcrust pastry for the casing
For the Filling:
2 lb. raisins
3 lb. currants
½ lb. chopped almonds
1 cup sugar
3 cups flour
2 teasp. allspice
1 teasp. ground ginger
¼ teasp. black pepper
1 teasp. ground cinnamon
1 teasp. cream of tartar
1 teasp. baking powder
1 tablsp. brandy
5 oz. milk

Mix all the filling ingredients together
except the milk. Add just enough milk to
moisten the mixture. Prepare the pastry
and roll out on floured board. Grease a
loaf tin 8 in. square and line with the
pastry, keeping enough aside for the top.
Fill the loaf tin with the mixture and put
the pastry lid on top, damping the edges to
make it stick. Prick all over with a fork,
and then with a thin skewer make four holes
down to the bottom of the cake. Brush with
beaten egg and cook in a slow (225F) oven for
about 3 hours.

FATTY CUTTIES

Fatty Cutties are like Northumbrian Singin'
Hinnies which were thought to 'sing' as they
cooked on the girdle because of the amount
of fat used.

6 oz. plain flour
pinch of baking soda
3 oz. currants
3 oz. melted butter
3 oz. sugar

Sift flour and baking soda together, then mix
in the currants and sugar. Add the melted
butter and mix together to make a stiff dough.
Place on a floured board and knead lightly till
smooth. Divide into two equal pieces and roll
out into a round about ¼" thick. Cut each
circle into 4 triangles and cook on a hot girdle
for about 5 minutes on each side until brown.
These should be served the same day as they are
baked.

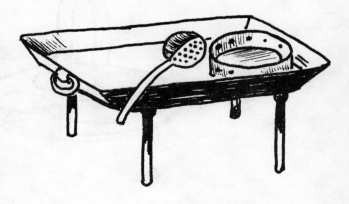

THE GIRDLE

Long before the day of the oven, the only
means of cooking were the pot and the girdle.
The girdle was, in fact, invented and first
used in Scotland in the late 16th century.
It has long been an important and traditional
piece of equipment in the Scots kitchen. It
is usually 14" across and made of cast iron.
The surface should never be washed but can be
rubbed with a coarse salt and then wiped with
a clean cloth. To prepare the surface for a
batter it should be greased lightly. The old
way was to wrap a piece of suet in muslin and
rub this over the surface when the girdle was
hot. Nowadays a piece of lard or some oil can
be rubbed in with a cloth kept specially for
this purpose. This is best done when the
girdle is hot. For bannocks, scones and
anything that is a dough, the surface should
be dusted lightly with flour. Heat the
girdle over a gentle heat.

SCOTS CRUMPETS

Scots Crumpets are also called 'Scots Pancakes'
and are made on a hot girdle or a lightly
greased, heavy pan.

½ lb. flour
2 eggs
2 tablsp. melted butter
3 tablsp. sugar
1 teasp. salt
15 oz. milk

Beat eggs well, then in another bowl mix flour,
sugar and salt, and add slowly melted butter
and eggs to flour mixture. Add enough milk to
make a thin creamy batter. Heat the girdle
and rub with a little oil, repeating as batter
is used. Beat batter well before using, and
then drop in large tablespoonfuls one at a time
on the girdle spreading it evenly. When golden
brown underneath, turn and cook on other side.
Set them on kitchen paper to drain and cover.
When cool spread with butter and jam, and
roll up. They should be served warm, soon
after making.

Makes about 20 pancakes.

ORKNEY PANCAKES

This is a variation of the Scots Crumpet
or Scots Pancake which is made with oatmeal
and buttermilk.

6 oz. oatmeal
2 tablsp. syrup
1¼ cups buttermilk
3 oz. self-raising flour
1 teasp. baking soda
1 egg

Place the oatmeal in a bowl and add the
buttermilk, mix thoroughly, cover and leave
overnight. Next day, sift flour and baking
soda. Stir in syrup, egg and enough milk
to make a thin consistency. Preheat girdle
and drop in tablespoonfuls on girdle,
browning on both sides. Place on cooking
rack. Serve warm with butter and honey.

BAPS

Baps are traditional yeast rolls, found all over Scotland, but Glasgow can be called the home of the tea-room during the 18th and 19th centuries.

1 lb. flour
1 oz. yeast
1 teasp. salt
1 teasp. sugar
2 tablsp. lard
1¼ cups warm milk

Mix the flour and salt in a warm bowl. Cream sugar and yeast together. Heat the lard and when melted add a little less than half the warm milk to it. Make a well in the middle of the flour and put in the yeast, milk and lard, and mix well. Knead until smooth, then cover and set in a warm place to rise for 1 hour. Knead lightly on floured board and then form into oval shapes about 3 in. long and 2 in. wide. Put on baking sheet, brush with milk, dust with a little flour. Leave again for 15 minutes, make a small dent in the middle of each Bap, and bake in hot (400F) oven for 15-20 minutes.

Makes about 10 Baps.

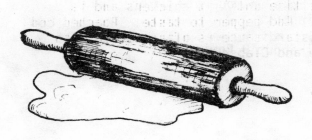

BUTTERY ROWIES

These are traditional Aberdeen butter yeast
rolls, which are folded into roughly-shaped
ovals. They are eaten warm, spread with
butter and marmalade.

1 lb. flour
1 oz. yeast
1 cup butter
½ cup lard
1 tablsp. sugar
15 oz. warm water
salt

Sift flour and pinch of salt then cream
the yeast with the sugar. When it bubbles
add to the flour with the water. Mix well,
cover and set in a warm place until double
in size, about ½hr. Cream the butter and
lard together and then divide into three.
Put the dough on a floured board and roll
out into long strips. Put the first third
of fat in dots on top third of pastry strip
and fold over like an envelope, as if
making flaky pastry. Roll out, and do
this twice more until all butter mixture is
used up. Roll out and cut into small oval
shapes or small rounds. Put on to a
floured baking sheet, leaving about 2 in.
between each one to allow for spreading.
Cover, and leave to rise for 3/4 hour,
then bake in moderate (375F) oven for
20 minutes.

Makes about 9 Rowies

CRULLAS

Crullas are small cakes or bannocks made into
a plait. The name comes from the Gaelic
'kril.' It is believed to have been introduced
to Scotland by the Dutch settlers and comes
from the Dutch 'krullen' meaning 'to curl.'

½ lb. plain flour
½ teasp. baking soda
2 oz. butter
2 oz. sugar
2 eggs
¼ teasp. cream of tartar
¼ teasp. salt
pinch of nutmeg or ginger
2½ oz. buttermilk
oil for frying

Cream the butter and sugar, then add the eggs,
flour, baking soda, cream of tartar, salt,
nutmeg or ginger. Add the buttermilk slowly,
mixing well, so the dough becomes firm. Place
on a floured board and roll into long strips.
Cut into 1 in. ribbons leaving the tops
together, and plait (braid) them, damping the
ends so they stick. Heat oil to 365F and fry
until golden brown. Drain on kitchen paper,
and sprinkle with fine sugar.

Makes about 1 dozen

The Scots are known to have a sweet tooth and are famous for their sweets (candies).

EDINBURGH ROCK

Edinburgh Rock has been made since the 18th Century and was first made popular by Alexander Ferguson.

1 lb. sugar   1 cup water
½ teasp. cream of tartar

Flavouring and colouring: a few drops

ginger (fawn), lemon (yellow), orange (orange or yellow), peppermint (green), raspberry (pink),vanilla (white).

Heat the sugar and water until the sugar dissolves. Just before it boils add the cream of tartar and boil without stirring until it reaches 250F, and sugar forms a hard ball in cold water. Remove from the heat and add the colouring you wish. Remember the colour will fade when the mixture is 'pulled.' Let mixture stand for a few minutes to cool slightly, then pour onto a buttered marble slab and turn the edges into the centre with an oiled scraper, but do not stir. When cool enough to handle, dust with icing sugar (confectioner's sugar) and 'pull' it evenly by holding it in your hands and letting it drop and then bringing it up again. Do not twist. Continue this process until it starts to harden then pull into one long strip about ½" thick. Cut the strip into 1-2 inch lengths with oiled scissors. Leave on greased paper for 24 hours to set,

when rock will become powdery and soft. It
can be stored in an air tight tin. If candy
remains sticky, it means that it has not beer
pulled enough.

BUTTERSCOTCH

2 lb. brown sugar
½ lb. butter
juice of 1 lemon

Dissolve sugar in a saucepan, and when liquid
add the butter and flavouring. Continue
boiling gently, stirring all the time for
about 20 minutes or until it hardens when a
little is dropped into water. Beat well for
5 minutes, pour on to a buttered slab, and
when cool mark into squares with a knife.
When cold and set, lift and tap the bottom
with a heavy knife handle to break up.

Makes about 2 lb. butterscotch.

TABLET or TAIBLET

This is a traditional Scots toffee and can
be flavoured according to taste with: clove,
cinnamon, ginger, lemon, orange, peppermint,
vanilla or nuts.

½ lb. butter
1¼ cups water
4 lb. sugar (extra fine)
1 lb. tin sweetened condensed milk

Place butter and water into a deep pan and
melt on low heat. When melted add the sugar
and bring to the boil, stirring slowly all
the time. When boiling, add the condensed
milk and simmer for 25 minutes, stirring
to prevent sticking. Remove from heat and

add the flavouring of your choice, then beat well for 5 minutes. Pour into a greased pan and mark into squares with a knife. Wrap pieces in waxed paper when cold.

Makes about 4 lb. of toffee

HELENSBURGH TOFFEE

This toffee is very popular in the Glasgow region and is a type of 'Tablet' or 'Taiblet.'

5 oz. water
2 lb. sugar
4 oz. butter
1 tablsp. syrup
1 cup condensed milk
vanilla extract
walnut halves

Make this toffee in the same way as the Tablet adding the vanilla flavouring and after marking into squares, when it has cooled a little press a walnut half on each square.

Makes about 2 lbs. of toffee

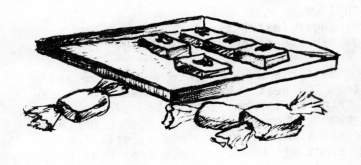

SWEET HAGGIS

Sweet Haggis is common to the Ayrshire region
and is quite often served for tea.

3/4 lb. medium oatmeal
½ cup plain flour
3/4 lb. suet, finely chopped
¼ cup currants
½ cup raisins
½ cup brown sugar
salt and pepper to taste
water to mix

Place all the ingredients in a bowl and mix
with water to blend mixture together without
making it wet. Place the mixture in a
greased pudding bowl, cover with foil or
greaseproof paper, tie, and steam for 3-4
hours. Serve hot in slices.

SWEET MARAGAN

This is another type of sweet haggis but is
a little heavier and comes from the Outer
Hebrides.

½ lb. oatmeal
½ lb. flour
2 oz. sugar
2 oz. raisins
½ cup finely chopped suet
salt and pepper to taste
1 teasp. onion, diced

Use the same method as Sweet Haggis. This can
be served hot, or if served cold, serve with
fried potatoes and bacon.

CLOUTIE DUMPLING

The name of this dish comes from the use
of a 'cloth' or 'clout' to boil the dumpling
in. They are very popular in the Highlands
at Hogmanay.

1 lb. plain flour
¼ cup breadcrumbs
¼ cup raisins
½ lb. sultanas
½ lb. currants
½ teasp. salt
2 teasp. each of cinnamon, mixed spice
                         and ginger
1 teasp. baking powder
2 cooking apples, grated
2 carrots, grated
2 eggs
½ lb. finely chopped suet
½ lb. brown sugar
¼ cup chopped mixed peel
½ lb. black treacle (molasses)
juice of 1 lemon or orange
milk to mix

Mix all the ingredients in a large bowl, using
milk to mix to a soft consistency. If you do
not have a boiling cloth the dumpling can also
be cooked in a greased pudding bowl. If a
pudding bowl is used the mixture should be
halved and two bowls, 7-cup size should be
used. Place half the mixture in a bowl
and cover with foil or greaseproof paper and
tie securely. Place the bowl in a saucepan
with the water about 3/4 of the way up the
bowl. Bring to simmering point, cover and
cook for about 3 hours. Check the water
level occasionally. Serve the dumpling on
a large warm plate and sprinkle with caster
sugar and eat hot with cream or custard.

GRANNY LOAF

This boiled fruit cake is very popular in the Highlands and probably came from the Cloutie Dumpling.

1 cup plain flour and 1 cup self-raising flour
3 oz. currants
3 oz. cut peel
3 oz. raisins
2 eggs
1 cup sugar
1 teasp. baking soda
1 teasp. mixed spice
3 oz. margarine
1 cup water

Place the water, sugar, margarine, mixed spice and fruit into a pan and bring to the boil. Simmer for a few minutes and then leave to cool. When cold add baking soda, eggs and sifted flours. Mix well. Place in a greased loaf tin, about 9" x 5". Bake in a moderate oven (350) for 1¼ hours.

BARLEY PUDDING

This is a Lothian dish and is eaten
with meat dishes. This recipe came from
an old dish called 'frumenty' or 'furmety'
which is hulled wheat boiled in milk and
seasoned with cinnamon, sugar and other
spices.

3 oz. barley
2 oz. currants
2½ cups water

Place barley in 5 cup ovenproof dish, cover
with water and bake for 3 hours in oven at
300F. Stir in currants for the last 20 minutes.
Serve with sugar and cream.

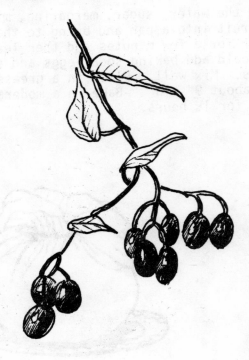

SKIRLIE

This was originally a cheap dish served with Chappit Tatties but it is now also served with chicken and game birds and roast meats. In some parts of Scotland it is called mealie pudding. Skirl means 'loud noise.'

2 cups medium oatmeal
½ cup grated suet
2 small onions, finely chopped
pepper

Melt suet in pan then add onions and lightly brown. Then stir in the oatmeal to make a thick mixture. Stir over gentle heat for 5-8 minutes until mixture is thoroughly cooked and add pepper to taste.

Serves 4-6

WHIPKULL

This is an old Shetland drink which is drunk at Christmas time for breakfast with a piece of shortbread. This drink is very similar to the Norwegian drink Eggedosis.

4 egg yolks
3 tablsp. rum
4 oz. sugar

Place the sugar in a double boiler, add the egg yolks and heat water in bottom of pan. Beat the sugar and egg yolks until thick and creamy then start to add the rum, beating all the time. Serve immediately whilst it is still warm, or it may be chilled for a few hours. Serve with a piece of shortbread.

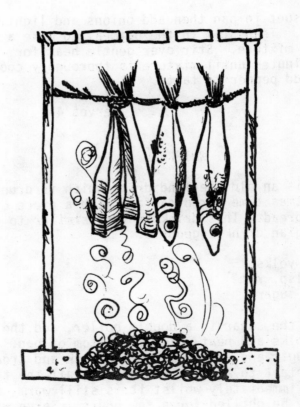

SCOTTISH BREAKFAST

The Scottish breakfast is usually a bowl of
porridge, which is made with salt and served
with cream or milk. (As my father was quick
to tell me, the use of sugar is severely
frowned upon.) Kippers are also considered
a favourite in Scotland. Kippers are
Herrings which have been split open before
curing. When they are cured closed they are
called 'Bloaters.' The flavour of the Kipper
depends upon the wood used to smoke it. Kippers
originated around Craster, on the Northumbrian
coast about 1840, where they were cured by a
secret oak-smoked process. The idea of curing
Herrings soon travelled north to Scotland where
they have an abundance of fish.

PORRIDGE

Porridge is the mainstay of Scotland. It is
usually made with oatmeal, but in the Orkney
and Shetland Isles it is made with bere-meal
(a type of barley). It also has different
names in various parts of the country. In the
Shetland Isles it is called "milgruel" and in
the Highlands it is called the Gaelic name
"brochan."

2½ cups cold water
2 oz. medium oatmeal
salt to taste

Bring the water to boil and add 1 teasp. salt.
Sprinkle the oatmeal slowly into the boiling
water, stirring constantly. Half cover the
saucepan and turn the heat down to low.
Stir occasionally until porridge thickens and
is creamy - about 30 minutes. Add more salt if
desired.

Serves approx. 4

TIPSY LAIRD

1 Angel Food Cake or Pound Cake
4 oz. Raspberry Jam
10 oz. Sherry
2-3 tablsp. Brandy
5 cups rich custard sauce
heavy cream
Ratafia biscuits (Almond cookies)
roasted almonds

Place ratafia biscuits around the base of
a glass bowl. Spread jam on cake and split
cake into small pieces and place on top of
ratafia biscuits. Mix sherry and brandy
together and pour over cake and allow to
soak thoroughly. 2 packages of Bird's
custard powder can be used if custard
sauce not available. Make custard and then
pour over sponge mixture and allow to cool.
Whip cream and pour over custard and
decorate with almonds.

Serves approx. 8-10

BREAD SAUCE

This sauce accompanies roast chicken, turkey or pheasant. To obtain a stronger onion flavour leave the onion in the sauce until serving.

1 onion
2 cups breadcrumbs
2 cups milk
2 cloves (optional)
1 oz. butter
1 bay leaf
salt and pepper to taste

Peel the onion, and if using cloves, stick them firmly into the onion. Put the onion in the milk together with the other ingredients. Slowly bring milk to the boil. Remove from heat and cover, and let stand 15-20 minutes. Just before serving, heat the sauce gently, then remove the onion before putting sauce into the sauce boat.

Serves approx. 6

THE HAGGIS

There is no dish so well-known as the HAGGIS.
Traditionally the Haggis is eaten at Burns
Suppers and St. Andrews night dinners, not
forgetting, of course, Hogmanay (New Year's
Eve). The Haggis was hailed by the poet
Robert Burns in his "Address to the Haggis"
as the 'Great Chieftain o' the puddin' race.'

Haggis is made from the pluck of a sheep
(stomach bag), which is then filled with a
mixture of finely chopped suet, toasted
oatmeal, liver, onion, stock and seasonings.
The Haggis is served with mashed potatoes
(Chappit Tatties) and mashed turnips (Neeps).
The custom is to take a sip of neat whisky
between each bite of Haggis. The Haggis is
brought into the dining room to the
accompaniment of bagpipes.

TO A HAGGIS

Fair fa' your honest, sonsie face,
Great Chieftain o' the Puddin-race,
Aboon them a' ye. tak your place,
Painch, tripe, or thairm,
Weel are ye wordy o' a grace
As lang's my arm.

***

Robert Burns

We have given you the traditional method of
making Haggis, but also a recipe for Quick
Haggis, which my mother made.

TRADITIONAL HAGGIS

1 sheep's pluck (stomach bag)
2 lbs dry oatmeal
1 lb suet
1 lb lamb's liver
2½ cups stock
1 large chopped onion
½ teasp. cayenne pepper, Jamaica pepper and salt

Boil liver and parboil the onion, then mince
them together. Lightly brown the oatmeal. Mix
all ingredients together. Fill the sheep's
pluck with the mixture, pressing it down to
remove all the air, and sew up securely. Prick
the Haggis in several places so that it does
not burst. Place Haggis in boiling water and
boil slowly for 4 to 5 hours.
Serves approximately 12

QUICK HAGGIS

½ lb. liver   ½ cup oatmeal   ½ cup suet
1 onion   5/8 cup stock
¼ teasp. cayenne pepper   ¼ teasp. salt

Boil the liver and parboil the onion, then
mince them together. Lightly brown the
oatmeal then mix all ingredients together.
Place in a greased basin and cover with foil,
or a suet crust if desired, and steam for
1½ hours. Serves 4

Haggis is often served with Chappit Tatties
and Neeps, but may also be served with
CLAPSHOT, which is a traditional dish from
the Orkney Isles.

CLAPSHOT

1 lb. potatoes
1 lb. turnips
1 tablsp. butter
1 tablsp. chopped chives
   or 4 scallions
salt and pepper to taste

Cook the vegetables separately, drain and
then mash then together very well, adding
all other ingredients. Season to taste
and serve hot.
Serves 4 to 6

93

ATHOLL BROSE

There are many stories of Atholl Brose, but one
well-known story tells how the Duke of Atholl,
during the Highland rebellion in 1475, captured
and defeated the rebel leader, Ian MacDonald,
the Earl of Ross, by filling the well Ross drank
from with a mixture of whisky, honey and meal.
Ross was so delighted with what he drank that he
stayed too long at the well allowing the Duke of
Atholl to capture him.

Atholl Brose is a favourite
drink on Hogmanay but may also
be used as a dessert.

6 oz. medium oatmeal
½ cup heather honey
30 oz. whisky
1 cup water

Put the oatmeal into a small
bowl, add water to make a paste.
Leave for about 1 hour then put
into a fine muslin or sieve and
press all the liquid through.
Add the honey to sieved liquid
and mix thoroughly. Pour into
a large bottle and fill up with
the whisky. Shake well. Keep
in cool place. Shake well
before use.

Atholl Brose as a dessert
could be called a Scottish
syllabub - meaning a dish made
of cream or milk curdled with
wine, etc., and sometimes
whipped or solidified with
gelatin. (A 16th Century word,
of unknown origin)

96

ATHOLL BROSE - A DESSERT

6 oz. heavy cream
½ cup oatmeal
½ cup heather honey
1 cup whisky

Whip heavy cream to a smooth consistency.
Lightly toast oatmeal and add to cream.
Stir in honey and whisky and mix
thoroughly. Serve in individual glass
dishes. You can decorate with strawberries
or raspberries if desired.

Serves 4

HET PINT

This drink was very popular in Glasgow and
Edinburgh at New Year about one hundred years
ago. It was made very hot and then carried
around the neighbourhood in a large kettle
and served to all the people.

10 cups of mild ale or red wine
1 teasp. grated nutmeg
3 eggs, beaten
1¼ cups whisky
½ cup sugar

Place the ale in a thick saucepan, and add
nutmeg, and bring to just under boiling-point.
stir in sugar and let it dissolve. Add the ·
beaten eggs very slowly, stirring all the time,
so that the mixture does not curdle. Then add
the whisky, and heat up, but do not boil. Serve
in beer tankards.

WHISKY PUNCH (cold)

5 cups water
1 bottle of Scotch whisky
3 lemons
½ lb. sugar

Peel lemons and squeeze out juice, then place
them in bowl with sugar. Boil water and pour
over lemons and sugar and leave until cold.
Strain into a large bowl and add the whisky,
stirring well. Serve chilled.

STOVED TATTIES or STOVIES

The potato is a basic vegetable used in many ways in Scotland. We believe Stovies came from the French étoufée, to stew in a closed vessel.

4-6 potatoes
salt and pepper to taste
1 large onion
2 oz. butter or meat drippings
1½ cups hot water or stock

Melt butter or drippings in pan. Peel and thickly slice the potatoes and onion and place in pan. Toss in the fat for a few minutes. Add the stock or water, salt and pepper. Cover and bring to the boil. Then simmer gently, stirring occasionally, until potatoes are soft and floury and the moisture almost absorbed. Serve with freshly chopped parsley.

Serves 4

NEEPS

1 large swede (turnip)
1 oz butter
salt and pepper to taste
pinch of grated nutmeg

Cut swede into large pieces, diced. Put in saucepan and cover with water, add salt. Cover and simmer until tender. Mash till smooth then add butter and nutmeg and salt and pepper to taste. These "bashed" neeps are served with Haggis.

Serves 2

SCOTCH WOODCOCK

This dish was traditionally served as a
savoury at the end of a meal, but nowadays
it is quite often served as a snack.

1 - 2oz. can anchovies in olive oil, drained
    and soaked in milk for 30 minutes
1 oz. butter
4 slices hot toast
3 eggs, beaten with 2 tablsp. milk
freshly ground black pepper
Cayenne pepper

Drain half of anchovies and mix with butter,
reserving a little butter for scrambling the
eggs. Spread the anchovy butter on the hot
toast and keep hot. Melt the remainder of the
butter in a saucepan and add the beaten eggs.
Season to taste with black pepper. Stir over
gentle heat until scrambled. Pile on the
buttered toast. Cut the remaining anchovy
fillets in half lengthways and use to decorate
in a lattice pattern on top of the scrambled
eggs. Sprinkle with cayenne pepper and serve
immediately.

Serves approx. 4

SCOTCH EGGS

Scotch Eggs, or as they are also referred
to 'Scots Eggs' are very popular. They make
a very good snack served with a crisp green
salad, and a glass of beer or lager.

1 lb. pork sausagemeat
1 teasp. mixed herbs
1 onion, finely chopped
flour for coating
1 egg, beated
about 6 oz. breadcrumbs
4 eggs hard-boiled and shelled
oil for deep-fat frying

Mix together the sausagemeat, mixed herbs
and onion. Divide the mixture into four
equal portions and mould firmly around the
eggs. Roll in flour, then dip in the
beaten egg. Coat with breadcrumbs, making
sure the eggs are evenly covered. Chill for
about 1 hr. before frying. Heat oil and fry
eggs for about 10 minutes until crisp and
golden-brown. Drain on kitchen paper.
When cool they may be cut in half and served
with a salad.

POTTED HOUGH

This traditional Scottish dish is eaten cold
with a salad or boiled potatoes.

2½-3 lb. hough (shank of beef)
salt and pepper to taste
pinch of mixed herbs
cold water

Place hough in saucepan with cold water -
enough to cover it. Add teasp. salt. Bring
to a slow boil and simmer gently for 5-6 hours,
then remove all the bones. Strain the meat and
place on a board. Mince the meat finely.
Return the meat to the stock. Add salt and
pepper to taste and herbs if required. Bring
quickly to the boil, and boil for 8-10 minutes.
Remove from stove and leave to cool, then
stir gently and put in greased mould to set.

THE FARIN'

"Some ha'e meat an' canna eat,
And some wad eat that want it,
But we ha'e meat an' we can eat,
And sae the Lord be thankit.

* * *

*
1759

+
1796

And if it please Thee, Heavenly Guide,
May never worse be sent:
But whether granted or denied,
Lord, bless us with content. "

Amen.

Robert Burns

AULD LANG SYNE

Should auld acquaintance be forgot,
  And never brought to mind,
Should auld acquaintance be forgot,
  And auld lang syne.

CHORUS-For auld lang syne, my dear,
      For auld lang syne,
    We'll tak a cup o' kindness yet
      For auld lang syne.

And surely ye'll be your pint stowp,
  And surely I'll be mine,
And we'll tak a cup o' kindness yet,
  For auld lang syne;

We twa hae run about the braes,
  And pou'd the gowans fine,
But we've wander'd mony a weary fitt,
  Sin' auld lang syne;

We twa hae paidl'd in the burn
  Frae morning sun till dine,
But seas between us braid hae roar'd,
  Sin' auld lang syne;

                ROBERT BURNS 1759-1796

The melody to which the song is now sung
was composed by William Shield, and forms
part of the overture to his opera 'Rosina'
(1783).   Some people sing 'kiss' in place
of 'cup' in the Chorus.